PLANET ROBO

VIMALRAJ.S

Contents

ABSTRACT

LIST OF FIGURES

LIST OF ABBRIVIATIONS

1. Introduction 7
2. Literature Survey 8
3. Block Diagram 9
4. Power Supply 11
5. Pic 16f877a Microcontroller 13
6. Uln2003 21
7. Video Camera 23
8. Encoders And Decoders 24
9. Zig-bee Module 25
10. Gsm 27
11. Lcd Display 29
12. Ultrasonic Sensor 30
13. Temperature Sensor 32
14. Water Probe Or Humidity Sensor 34
15. Light-dependent Resistor (ldr) 35
16. Pc Controlling 37
17. Hardware Results 38
18. Cost Estimation 39
19. Appendix 40
20. Conclusion 48

ABSTRACT

Wireless Robotics is one of the emerging field in the world of automation. Robots have found applications in many domain including industrial automation, health-care, surveillance, planetary exploration or rescue missions.

This project is to design the robot for the researching the other planet to get various information and data analyzing.

We are using the computer in this project to control the Robot for data detection through the wireless camera and various sensors. For controlling the robot, the signal is transmitted through the Zig-Bee using computer.

The principle of task of the project was to program the PIC16f877A microcontroller interfaced to a Zig-Bee

Which would enable us to wirelessly control the robot. The communication dealing is successfully implemented using the various types of sensors. These details are discussed in this report

LIST OF FIGURES

Fig 1. Block diagram1

Fig 2. Block diagram2

Fig 3. Power supply

Fig 4. Circuit diagram(power supply)

Fig 5. Pin diagram of PIC16f877A

Fig 6. Architecture of PIC16f877A

Fig 7. Pin out description of PIC16f877A

Fig 8. Motor driver ULN2003

Fig 9. Zig-Bee module

Fig 10. GSM module

Fig 11. Ultrasonic Sensor HC SR-04

Fig 12. Temperature sensor

Fig 13. Humidity sensor

Fig 14. LDR sensor

LIST OF ABBRIVIATIONS

PIC - Peripheral Interface Controller

RISC - Reduced Instruction Set Computing

EEPROM - Electronically Erasable Programmable ROM

GSM - Global System for Mobile communication

LCD - Liquid Crystal Display

LDR - Light Dependent Resistor

USART - Universal synchronous asynchronous receiver/transmitter

CMOS - Complementary Metal Oxide Semiconductor

LED - Light Emitting Diode

1

INTRODUCTION

This is being a model robot. So here so many advantages and advancements are added to smart the work easily without human stress. Now a days the robots are playing very important role in automation of companies. This is to reduce the human error and too increase the productivity.

The aim of the project is to build a planet research robot using wireless technology in PC. Our project is to design the Robot for the researching the other planet to get various information and data analyzing.

We are using the computer in this project to control the Robot for data detection through the wireless video camera and various sensors. For controlling the robot, the signal is transmitted through the zig-bee using computer. We can use any software to control the Robot like VB, .NET, Lab VIEW etc.

Here shielding the robot can withstand various environmental conditions such as high temperature, pressure, wind, humidity, water etc. attaching cameras also be helpful in tracking the location of the robot. In order to move on heavy rocky substances or on areas like slope there may be chances of getting tumble top of the robot hence gripper tyres can be fitted so that it can move easily over heavy substances.

2

LITERATURE SURVEY

Robotics as a research field has been to develop the fundamental building blocks to allow autonomous operation, mobility, localization, mapping and control. The advancement in each of these area have been incredible. Planet research robot is an extension and application to these fundamental robotic research areas. The heritage of planet research robot has been to explore particularly challenging natural environment. The early robotic system were developed to follow the preset mission plans and capture data that was retrieved after the experiment.

They proved research into integrated system design, global positioning system - denied navigation, mission and path planning could allow capture of accurately localized environmental data in harsh environment over an extended period of time.

In our project we have advanced live telecasting through video and can take required information through GSM at any instant of time. The pictures taken at the time of monitoring can be viewed instantly unlike other robots which cannot be viewed at preferable time.

3
BLOCK DIAGRAM

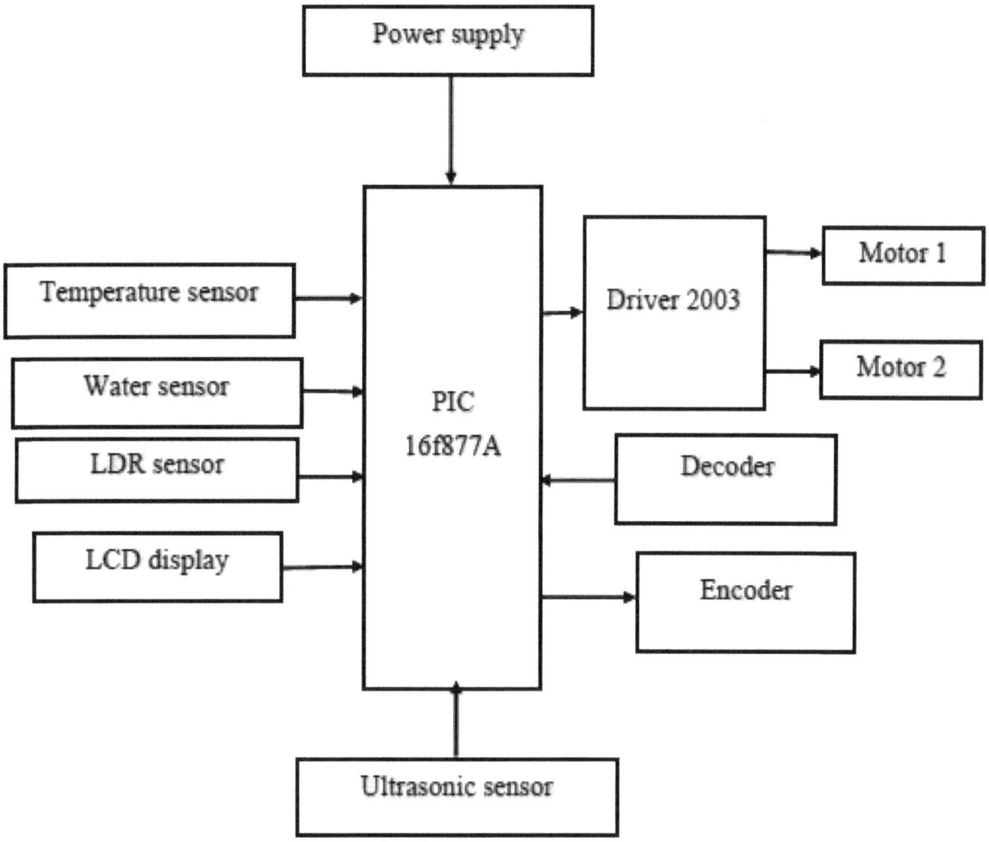

Fig 1. Block diagram 1

3.1. EARTH (RECEIVING STATION):

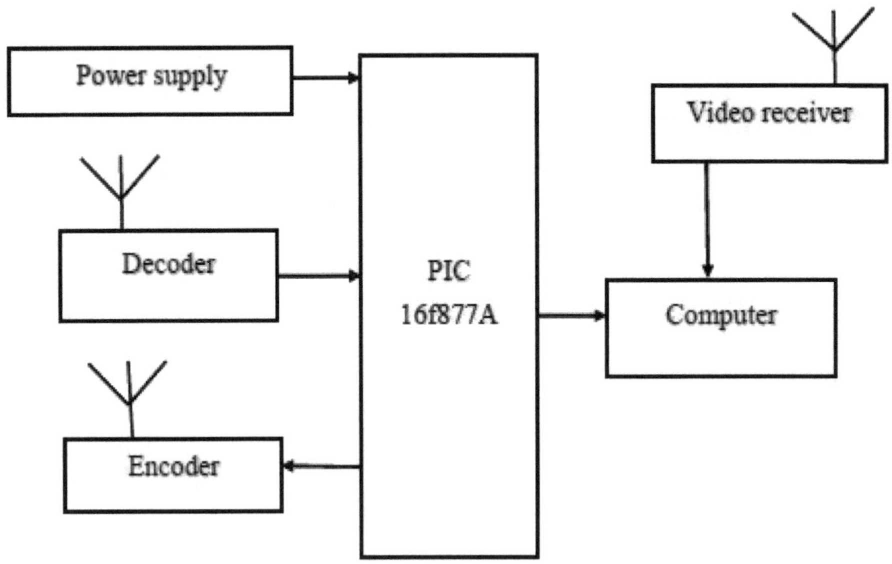

Fig 1. Block diagram 2

4

POWER SUPPLY

4.1 Scope:

Power supply is a reference to a source of electrical power. A device or system that supplies electrical or other types of energy to an output load or group of loads is called a power supply unit. The term is most commonly applied to electrical energy supplies, less often to mechanical ones, and rarely to others.

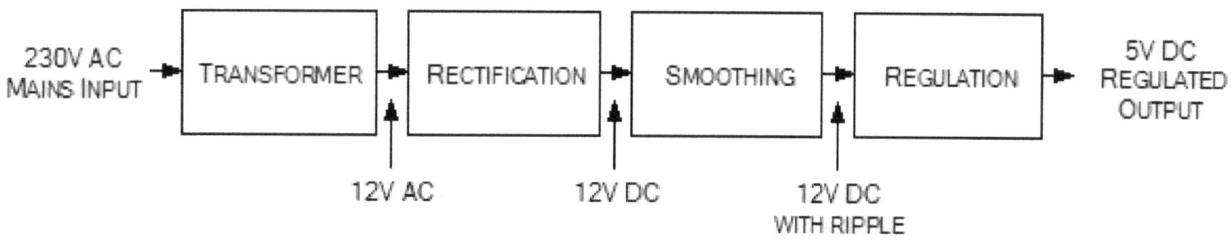

Fig 3. Block diagram(Power supply)

This typically involves converting 240 volt AC supplied by a utility company to a well-regulated lower voltage (+/-12V) DC for electronic devices.

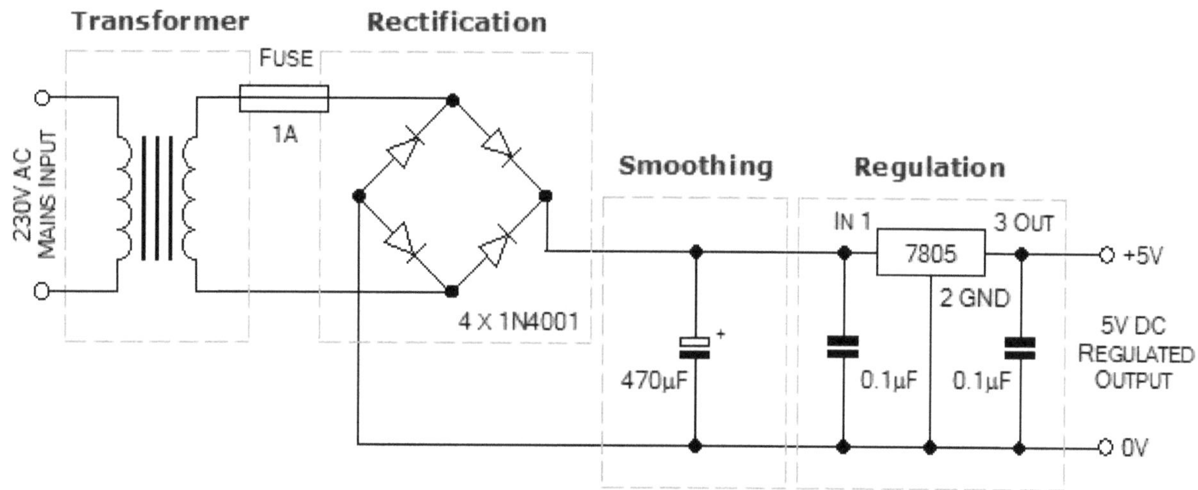

Fig 4. Circuit diagram (power supply)

The ac voltage, typically 220V rms, is connected to a transformer, which steps that ac voltage down to the level of the desired dc output. A diode rectifier then provides a full-wave rectified voltage that is initially filtered by a simple capacitor filter to produce a dc voltage. This resulting dc voltage usually has some ripple or ac voltage variation.

A regulator circuit removes the ripples and also remains the same dc value even if the input dc voltage varies, or the load connected to the output dc voltage changes. This voltage regulation is usually obtained using one of the popular voltage regulator IC units.

5

PIC 16F877A MICROCONTROLLER

5.1 CORE FEATURES

- High-performance RISC CPU
- Only 35 single word instructions to learn
- All single cycle instructions except for program branches which are two cycle
- Operating speed: DC - 20 MHz clock input DC - 200 ns instruction cycle Up to 8K x 14 words of Flash Program Memory, Up to 368 x 8 bytes of Data Memory (RAM)

Up to 256 x 8 bytes of EEPROM data memory

- Pin out compatible to the PIC16C73/74/76/77
- Interrupt capability (up to 14 internal/external
- Eight level deep hardware stack
- Direct, indirect, and relative addressing modes
- Power-on Reset (POR)
- Power-up Timer (PWRT) and Oscillator Start-up Timer (OST)
- Watchdog Timer (WDT) with its own on-chip RC Oscillator for reliable operation
- Programmable code-protection
- Power saving SLEEP mode
- Selectable oscillator options
- Low-power, high-speed CMOS EPROM/EEPROM technology
- Fully static design
- In-Circuit Serial Programming (ICSP) via two pins
- Only single 5V source needed for programming capability

5.2 PIN DIAGRAM OF PIC 16F877

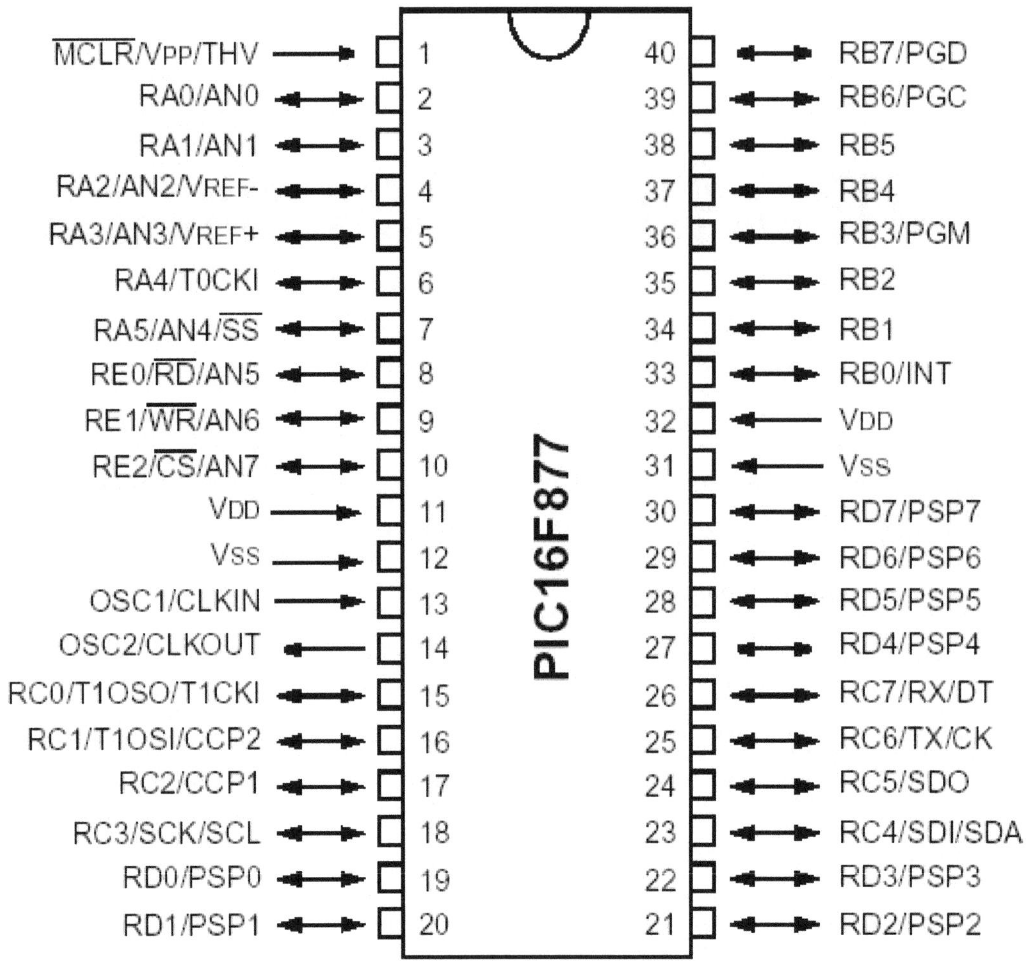

Fig 5. Pin diagram of PICF877A

5.3 ARCHITECTURE OF PIC 16F877A

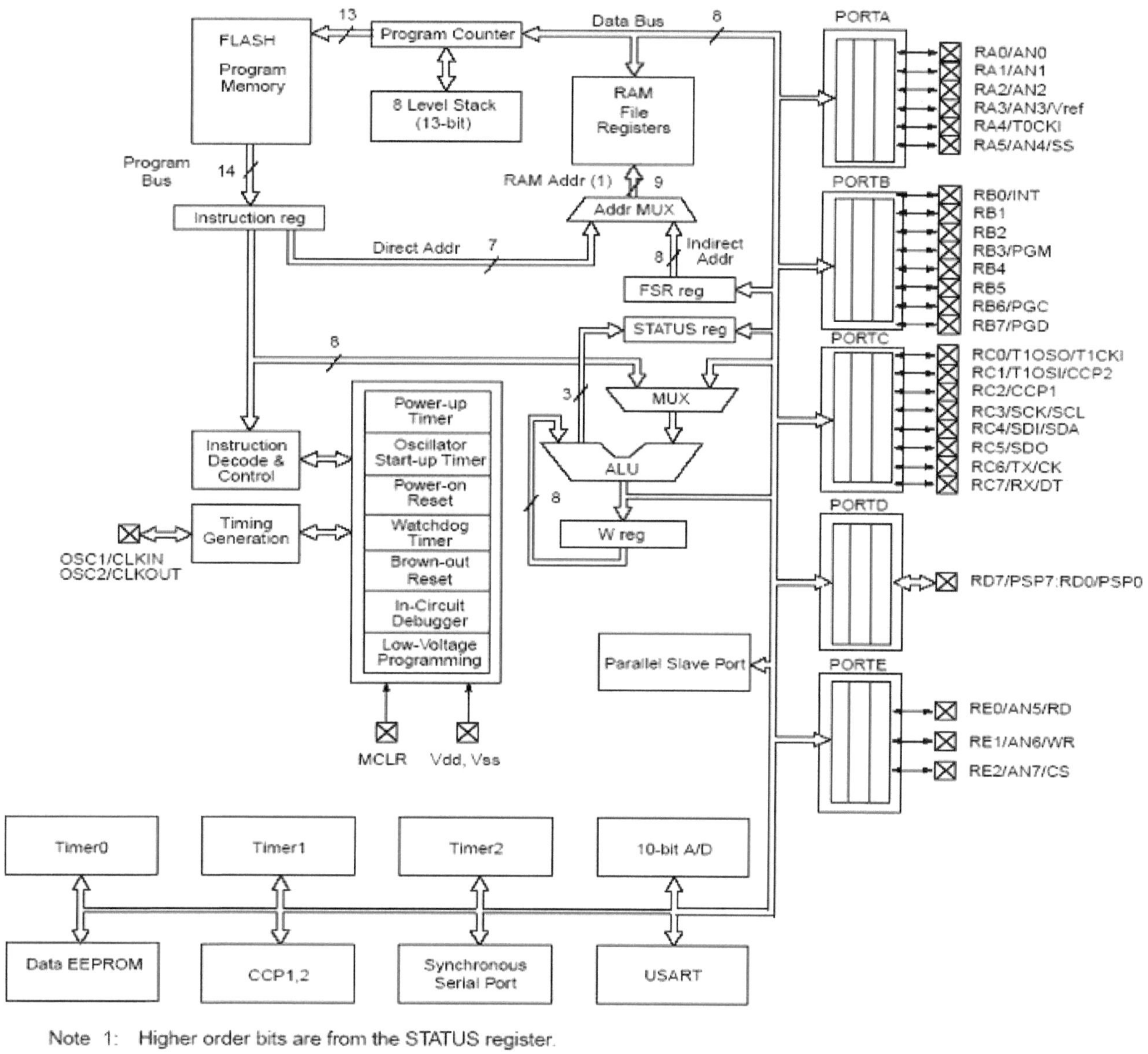

Fig 6. Architecture of PIC 16F877A

5.4 PIN DESCRIPTION

Pin Name	DIP Pin#	PLCC Pin#	QFP Pin#	I/O/P Type	Buffer Type	Description
OSC1/CLKIN	13	14	30	I	ST/CMOS(4)	Oscillator crystal input/external clock source input.
OSC2/CLKOUT	14	15	31	O	—	Oscillator crystal output. Connects to crystal or resonator in crystal oscillator mode. In RC mode, OSC2 pin outputs CLKOUT which has 1/4 the frequency of OSC1, and denotes the instruction cycle rate.
$\overline{\text{MCLR}}$/VPP/THV	1	2	18	I/P	ST	Master clear (reset) input or programming voltage input or high voltage test mode control. This pin is an active low reset to the device.
						PORTA is a bi-directional I/O port.
RA0/AN0	2	3	19	I/O	TTL	RA0 can also be analog input0
RA1/AN1	3	4	20	I/O	TTL	RA1 can also be analog input1
RA2/AN2/VREF-	4	5	21	I/O	TTL	RA2 can also be analog input2 or negative analog reference voltage
RA3/AN3/VREF+	5	6	22	I/O	TTL	RA3 can also be analog input3 or positive analog reference voltage
RA4/T0CKI	6	7	23	I/O	ST	RA4 can also be the clock input to the Timer0 timer/counter. Output is open drain type.
RA5/$\overline{\text{SS}}$/AN4	7	8	24	I/O	TTL	RA5 can also be analog input4 or the slave select for the synchronous serial port.
						PORTB is a bi-directional I/O port. PORTB can be software programmed for internal weak pull-up on all inputs.
RB0/INT	33	36	8	I/O	TTL/ST(1)	RB0 can also be the external interrupt pin.
RB1	34	37	9	I/O	TTL	
RB2	35	38	10	I/O	TTL	
RB3/PGM	36	39	11	I/O	TTL	RB3 can also be the low voltage programming input
RB4	37	41	14	I/O	TTL	Interrupt on change pin.
RB5	38	42	15	I/O	TTL	Interrupt on change pin.
RB6/PGC	39	43	16	I/O	TTL/ST(2)	Interrupt on change pin or In-Circuit Debugger pin. Serial programming clock.
RB7/PGD	40	44	17	I/O	TTL/ST(2)	Interrupt on change pin or In-Circuit Debugger pin. Serial programming data.

Pin Name	DIP Pin#	PLCC Pin#	QFP Pin#	I/O/P Type	Buffer Type	Description
						PORTC is a bi-directional I/O port.
RC0/T1OSO/T1CKI	15	16	32	I/O	ST	RC0 can also be the Timer1 oscillator output or a Timer1 clock input.
RC1/T1OSI/CCP2	16	18	35	I/O	ST	RC1 can also be the Timer1 oscillator input or Capture2 input/Compare2 output/PWM2 output.
RC2/CCP1	17	19	36	I/O	ST	RC2 can also be the Capture1 input/Compare1 output/ PWM1 output.
RC3/SCK/SCL	18	20	37	I/O	ST	RC3 can also be the synchronous serial clock input/ output for both SPI and I^2C modes.
RC4/SDI/SDA	23	25	42	I/O	ST	RC4 can also be the SPI Data In (SPI mode) or data I/O (I^2C mode).
RC5/SDO	24	26	43	I/O	ST	RC5 can also be the SPI Data Out (SPI mode).
RC6/TX/CK	25	27	44	I/O	ST	RC6 can also be the USART Asynchronous Transmit or Synchronous Clock.
RC7/RX/DT	26	29	1	I/O	ST	RC7 can also be the USART Asynchronous Receive or Synchronous Data.
						PORTD is a bi-directional I/O port or parallel slave port when interfacing to a microprocessor bus.
RD0/PSP0	19	21	38	I/O	ST/TTL[3]	
RD1/PSP1	20	22	39	I/O	ST/TTL[3]	
RD2/PSP2	21	23	40	I/O	ST/TTL[3]	
RD3/PSP3	22	24	41	I/O	ST/TTL[3]	
RD4/PSP4	27	30	2	I/O	ST/TTL[3]	
RD5/PSP5	28	31	3	I/O	ST/TTL[3]	
RD6/PSP6	29	32	4	I/O	ST/TTL[3]	
RD7/PSP7	30	33	5	I/O	ST/TTL[3]	
						PORTE is a bi-directional I/O port.
RE0/$\overline{RD}$/AN5	8	9	25	I/O	ST/TTL[3]	RE0 can also be read control for the parallel slave port, or analog input5.
RE1/$\overline{WR}$/AN6	9	10	26	I/O	ST/TTL[3]	RE1 can also be write control for the parallel slave port, or analog input6.
RE2/$\overline{CS}$/AN7	10	11	27	I/O	ST/TTL[3]	RE2 can also be select control for the parallel slave port, or analog input7.
V_{SS}	12,31	13,34	6,29	P	—	Ground reference for logic and I/O pins.
V_{DD}	11,32	12,35	7,28	P	—	Positive supply for logic and I/O pins.
NC	—	1,17,28, 40	12,13, 33,34		—	These pins are not internally connected. These pins should be left unconnected.

Pin Name	DIP Pin#	PLCC Pin#	QFP Pin#	I/O/P Type	Buffer Type	Description
OSC1/CLKIN	13	14	30	I	ST/CMOS(4)	Oscillator crystal input/external clock source input.
OSC2/CLKOUT	14	15	31	O	—	Oscillator crystal output. Connects to crystal or resonator in crystal oscillator mode. In RC mode, OSC2 pin outputs CLKOUT which has 1/4 the frequency of OSC1, and denotes the instruction cycle rate.
$\overline{\text{MCLR}}$/VPP/THV	1	2	18	I/P	ST	Master clear (reset) input or programming voltage input or high voltage test mode control. This pin is an active low reset to the device.
						PORTA is a bi-directional I/O port.
RA0/AN0	2	3	19	I/O	TTL	RA0 can also be analog input0
RA1/AN1	3	4	20	I/O	TTL	RA1 can also be analog input1
RA2/AN2/VREF-	4	5	21	I/O	TTL	RA2 can also be analog input2 or negative analog reference voltage
RA3/AN3/VREF+	5	6	22	I/O	TTL	RA3 can also be analog input3 or positive analog reference voltage
RA4/T0CKI	6	7	23	I/O	ST	RA4 can also be the clock input to the Timer0 timer/counter. Output is open drain type.
RA5/$\overline{\text{SS}}$/AN4	7	8	24	I/O	TTL	RA5 can also be analog input4 or the slave select for the synchronous serial port.
						PORTB is a bi-directional I/O port. PORTB can be software programmed for internal weak pull-up on all inputs.
RB0/INT	33	36	8	I/O	TTL/ST(1)	RB0 can also be the external interrupt pin.
RB1	34	37	9	I/O	TTL	
RB2	35	38	10	I/O	TTL	
RB3/PGM	36	39	11	I/O	TTL	RB3 can also be the low voltage programming input
RB4	37	41	14	I/O	TTL	Interrupt on change pin.
RB5	38	42	15	I/O	TTL	Interrupt on change pin.
RB6/PGC	39	43	16	I/O	TTL/ST(2)	Interrupt on change pin or In-Circuit Debugger pin. Serial programming clock.
RB7/PGD	40	44	17	I/O	TTL/ST(2)	Interrupt on change pin or In-Circuit Debugger pin. Serial programming data.

Fig 7. Pin out description

Legend: I = input O = output I/O = input/output P = power= Not used TTL = TTL input ST = Schmitt Trigger input

Note

1. This buffer is a Schmitt Trigger input when configured as an external interrupt.
2. This buffer is a Schmitt Trigger input when used in serial programming mode and This buffer is a Schmitt Trigger input when configured as general purpose I/O and a TTL input when used in the Parallel Slave Port mode (for interfacing to a microprocessor bus).

5.5 MEMORY ORGANISATION

There are three memory blocks in each of the PIC16F877 MUC's. The program memory and Data Memory have separate buses so that concurrent access can occur.

5.5.1 PROGRAM MEMORY ORGANISATION

RP1:RP0	BANKS
00	0
01	1
10	2
11	3

The PIC16f877 devices have a 13-bit program counter capable of addressing 8K *14 words of FLASH program memory. Accessing a location above the physically implemented address will cause a wraparound. The RESET vector is at 0000h and the interrupt vector is at 0004h.Table 3.3 shows the data memory organization.

5.5.2 DATA MEMORY ORGANIZATION

The data memory is partitioned into multiple banks which contain the General Purpose Registers and the special functions Registers. Bits RP1 (STATUS<6) each bank extends up to 7Fh (1238 bytes). The lower locations of each bank are reserved for the Special Function Registers. Above the Special Function Registers are General and RP0 (STATUS<5>) are the bank selected its.

5.6 TIMERS

There are three timers used Timer 0, Timer1 and Timer2

5.6.1 Timer-0

- 8-bit timer/counter
- software programmable prescaler
- Internal or external clock select
- Readable writable
- Interrupt on overflow

5.6.2 Timer-1

- It is 16-bit register
- software programmable prescaler
- Interrupt on overflow
- Readable and writable

The timer-1 module is a 16-bit timer/counter consisting two 8-bit register (TMR1H) and TMR1L), which are readable and writable. The TMR1 register pair (TMR1H:TMR1L) Increments from 0000h to FFFFH and rolls over to 0000h.

5.6.3 Timer-2

- Timer2 is an 8-bit timer with a prescaler and a postscaler. IT can be used as the PWM.
- Time-base for the PWM mode of the CCP module(s). The TMR2 register is readable and writable, and is cleared on any device reset.
- The input clock (Fosc/4) has a prescale option of 1:1, 1:4 OR 1:16, selected by control bits.

- The timer2 module has an 8-bit period register PR2. Timer2 increments from 00h until it match PR2 and then resets to 00h on the next increment cycle. PR2 is a readable and writable register. The PR2 register is initialized to FFh upon reset.

5.7 ANALOG TO DIGITAL CONVERTER (ADC)

There are two types of analog to digital converter is present in this IC. We use 10-bit ADC. The ADC module can have up to eight analog inputs for a device. The analog input charges a sample and hold capacitor. The output of sample and hold capacitor is the input into the converter. The converter then generates a digital result of this analog level via successive approximation. The A/D conversion of the analog input signal results in a corresponding10-bit digital number. The A/D module has high and low voltage reference input that is software selectable to some combination of VDD, VSS, and RA2 or RA3.

5.8 INTERRUPTS

The PIC16F87X has up to 14 sources of interrupt. The interrupt control register (INTCON) records individual interrupt requests in flag bits. IT also has individual interrupt requests in flag bits. IT also has individual and global interrupt enables bits. Though some modules may generate multiple interrupts such as (USART) they have 14 sources.

5.8 INTCON

Additionally if the device has peripheral interrupts to hold the interrupt flag bits

1. PIE1
2. PIR1
3. PIE2
4. PIR2

6

ULN2003

Fig 8. Motor driver ULN2003

ULN2003 is high voltage and high current Darlington array IC. It contains seven open collector Darlington pairs with common emitters. A Darlington pair is an arrangement of two bipolar transistors. ULN2003 belongs to the only of ULN200x series of IC's. Different versions of this family is interface to different logic families. ULN2003 has 2.7 kilo ohm series resistor for each Darlington pair for operation directly with TTL or 5V CMOS devices. These ICs are used when driving a wide range of loads and used as relay drivers, display drivers, line drivers etc. ULN2003 is also commonly used while driving the motors.Each channel or Darlington pair in ULN2003 is rated at 500 MA can withstand peak current of 600 m. the inputs and outputs are provided opposite to each other in the pin layout.

6.1 Features:

- Rated collector current 500mA(single output)
- High-voltage outputs:50V
- Inputs compatible with various types of logic
- Relay driver application

6.2 Pin description:

Pin no	Function	Name
1	Input for channell	Input 1
2	Input for channell	Input 2
3	Input for channell	Input 3
4	Input for channell	Input 4
5	Input for channell	Input 5
6	Input for channell	Input 6
7	Input for channell	Input 7
8	Ground (0V)	Ground
9	Common free wheeling diodes	Common
10	Output for channel 7	Output 7
11	Output for channel 7	Output 6
12	Output for channel 7	Output 5
13	Output for channel 7	Output 4
14	Output for channel 7	Output 3
15	Output for channel 7	Output 2
16	Output for channel 7	Output 1

7

VIDEO CAMERA

The C3088 camera operates at a voltage of 5V. It has a built in crystal that oscillates at 17.73MHz. It is capable of taking relatively high resolution images at 101,376 pixels. The difference in operating voltage between the camera (at 5V) and the rest of the circuit (at 3.6V) does not pose an issue because only the camera's digital IO pins are receiving signals from the rest of the system's circuit. The camera's digital IO pins used for I2C communication are able to accept lower range of voltage values at 3.6V from the MCU GPIO pins. The image data received by the MCU, no doubt has a maximum voltage level of 5V, can still be handled appropriately by the MCU.

7.1FEATURES:

- Powerful high-speed video protocol processor
- High-sensitivity 1/4" CMOS sensor
- 300K Pixels
- IR night vision(Range:3~5m)
- Optimized MJPEG video compression for transmission
- Multi-level users management and passwords definition
- Embedded Web Server for users to visit by IE
- Support wireless network (Wi-Fi/802.11/b/g)mobile
- Giving alarm in cause of motion detection
- Support one-way (I/O) alarm connection
- Support one-way Audio surveillance
- Supporting image snapshot
- Support remote system update

8

ENCODERS AND DECODERS

8.1 DECODERS:

The decoders receive serial addresses and data from a programmed 2^12 series of encoders that are transmitted by a carrier using an RF or an IR transmission medium. They compare the serial input data three times continuously with their local addresses. If no error or unmatched codes are found, the input data codes are decoded and then transferred to the output pins. The VT pin also goes high to indicate a valid transmission. The 2^12 series of decoders are capable of decoding information's that consist of N bits of address and 12_N bits of data. Of this series, the HT12D is arranged to provide 8 address bits and 4 data bits, and HT12F is used to decode 12 bits of address information.

8.2 FEATURES:

1. 18-pin DIP, 20-pin SOP package
2. Address/data number combinations

    - HT12D: 8 address bits and 4 data bits
    - HT122f: 12 address bits only

3. Low power and high noise immunity CMOS technology
4. Low standby current
5. Operating voltage: 2.4V to 12V

8.2 ENCODERS:

The 212 encoders are a series of CMOS LSIs for remote control system applications. They are capable of encoding information which consists of N address bits and 12_N data bits. Each address/ data input can be set to one of the two logic states. The programmed addresses/data are transmitted together with the header bits via an RF or an infrared transmission medium upon receipt of a trigger signal. The capability to select a TE trigger on the HT12E or a DATA trigger on the HT12A further enhances the application flexibility of the 212 series of encoders. The HT12A additionally provides a 38 kHz carrier for infrared systems.

8.2 EFeatures:

- Operating voltage: 2.4 to 5V for HT12A and 2.4V to 12V for HT12E
- Low power and high noise immunity CMOS technology.
- Low standby current: 0.1μA(typ.) at VDD= 5V

9

ZIG-BEE MODULE

Fig 9. Zig-bee module

CC2500 RF Module is a transreceiver module which provides easy to use RF communication at 2.4 Ghz. It can be used to transmit and receive data at 9600 baud rates from any standard CMOS/TTL source. This module is a direct line in replacement for your serial communication it requires no extra hardware and no extra coding toIt works in Half Duplex mode i.e. it provides communication in both directions, but only one direction at same time

Features:

- Supports Multiple Baud rates (9600)

- Works on ISM band (2.4 GHz)
- No complex wireless connection software or intimate knowledge of RF is required to connect our serial devices.
- Designed to be aseasy to use as cables.
- No external Antenna required.
- Plug and play device.
- Works on 5 DC supply.

Specifications:

- Input Voltage - 5Volts DC
- Baud Rate - 9600
- RS 232 Interface & TTL Interface
- Range – Max 30 Mtrs - Line of Sight
- Channels - 3 Ch - JP1 & JP2 - Ch 1 On – On

CC2500 RF Module
Channel Setting - If U need To use More than 2 Xbee in the same place So U can set in Diffrent
Channels - settings Given Below - JP1 and JP2 is nearby Chip in BOT Layer PCB

CHANNELS	JP1	JP2
CH1	OFF	OFF
CH2	ON	OFF
CH3	OFF	ON

Applications:

- Wireless Sensor Network.
- Wireless Device Control.
- Wireless Data Transfer.
- Wireless Energy Metering
- Home Automation

10

GSm

This is plug and play GSM Modem with a simple to interface serial interface. use it to a SMS, make and receive calls, as well as DATA transfer application and do other GSM operations by controlling through simple AT commands from microcontrollers and computers. It uses the highly popular SIM900a module for all its operations.

This GSM/GPRS TTL modem has internal TCP/IP stack to enable user to connect with a internet through GPRS feature. This modes can be interfaced with a microcontroller using USART.

The modem consists of all the required external circuitry required to start experimenting with the SIM900a module like the power regulation, external antenna, SIM holder.

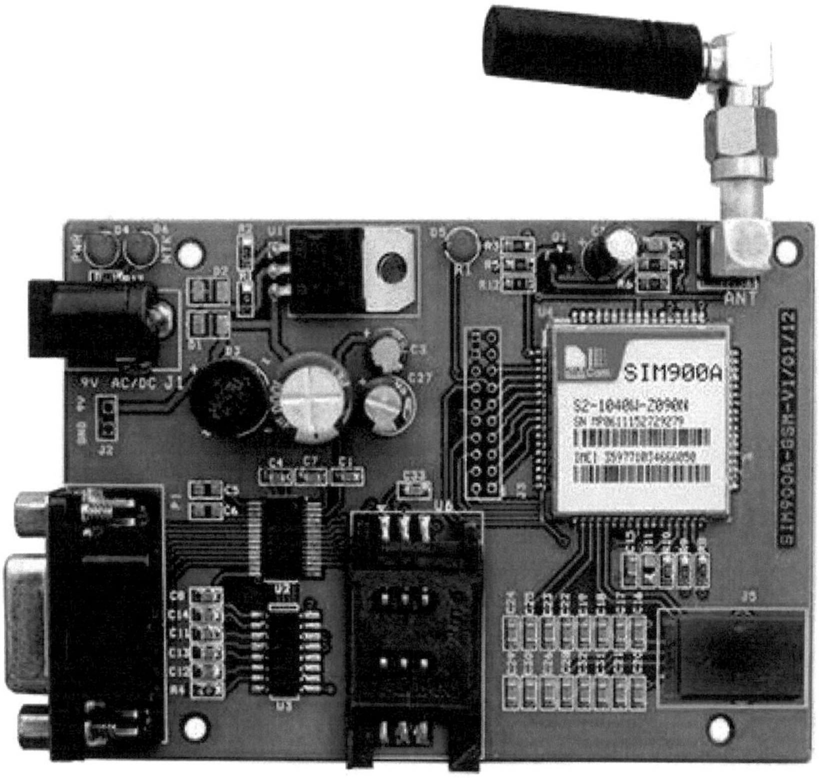

Fig 10. GSM module

10:1 **Features:**

- Quad band GSM/GPRS : 850/900/18001900 MHz

- Provides the industry standard serial RS332 interface foe easy connection to computers and other devices
- Built in RS232 to TTL or viceversa Logic convertor(MAX232)
- Built in Network status LED
- Onboard 3V lithium battery holder with appropriate circuitry for providing backup for modules' internal RTC
- Audio interface connectors(Audio in Audio out)
- SMA connector with GSM L type Antenna.
- Input voltage : 5V to 12V DC
- Normal operation temperature : -20 to +55 degree calicoes
- Module operation mode can be controlled through PWR switch connected to the PWR pin (refer the sim900a datasheet for more information)

11

LCD DISPLAY

Liquid crystal displays (LCDs) have materials which combine the properties of both liquids and crystals. Rather than having a melting point, they have a temperature range within which the molecules are almost as mobile as they would be in a liquid, but are grouped together in an ordered form similar to a crystal.

An LCD consists of two glass panels, with the liquid crystal material sand switched in between them. The inner surface of the glass plates are coated with transparent electrodes which define the character, symbols or patterns to be displayed polymeric layers are present in between the electrodes and liquid crystal, which makes the liquid crystal molecules to maintain a defined orientation angle.

Each polarizer's are pasted outside the two glass panels. This polarizer would rotate the light rays passing through them to a definite angle, in a particular direction.

When the LCD is in the off state, light rays are rotated by the two polarizer and liquid crystal, such that the light rays come out of the LCD without any orientation, and hence the LCD appears transparent.

When sufficient voltage is applied to the electrodes, the liquid crystal molecules would be aligned in a specific direction. The light rays passing through the LCD would be rotated by the polarizer's, which would result in activating/highlighting the desired characters.

The LCD's are light weight with only a few millimeters thickness. Since the LCD's consume less power, they are compatible with low power electronic circuits, and can be powered for long durations.

The LCD doesn't generate light and so light is needed to read the display. By using backlighting, reading is possible in dark. The LCD's have long life and a wide operating temperature range.

Changing the display size or the layout size is relatively simple which makes the LCD's more customer friendly.

The LCD's used exclusively in watches, calculators and measuring instruments are the seven segment displays, having a limited amount of numeric data. The recent advance in technology have resulted in better legibility, more information displaying capability and a wider temperature range.

12

ULTRASONIC SENSOR

Ultrasonic sensor are devices that use electrical–mechanical energy transformation to measure distance from the sensor to the target object. Ultrasonic waves are longitudinal mechanical waves which travel as a sequence of compressions and rarefactions along the direction of wave propagation through the medium. Apart from distance measurement, they are also used in ultrasonic material testing (to detect cracks, air bubbles, and other flaws in the products), Object detection, position detection, ultrasonic mouse, etc.

These sensors are categorized in two types according to their working phenomenon – piezoelectric sensors and electrostatic sensors. Here we are discussing the **ultrasonic sensor using the piezoelectric principle. Piezoelectric ultrasonic sensors** use a piezoelectric material to generate the ultrasonic waves.

Fig 11. Ultrasonic Sensor HC SR-04

HC SR-04 - Product features:

Ultrasonic ranging module HC - SR04 provides 2cm - 40cm the ranging accuracy can reach to 3mm. The modules includes ultrasonic transmitter, receiver and control circuit. The basic principle of work:

1. Using IO trigger for at least 10us high level signal,
2. The Module automatically sends eight 40 kHz and detect whether there is a pulse signal back.

3. IF the signal back, through high level , time of high output IO duration is the time from sending ultrasonic to returning.Test distance = (high level time×velocity of sound (340M/S) / 2.

   Easy to Interface conversion boads avilable now (PWM TO UART , OBSTACLE) - based on PIC microcontroller

- OBSTACLE INTEFACE BRD
- UART & OBSTACLE O/P BRD

Interfacing Pins:

1. 5V Supply
2. Trigger Pulse Input 3)Echo Pulse Output 4)0V Ground

Electric Parameters:

- Working Voltage DC 5 V
- Working Current 15mA
- Working Frequency 40Hz
- Max Range 40cm
- Min Range 2cm
- Measuring Angle 15 degree
- Trigger Input Signal 10uS TTL pulse
- Echo Output Signal Input TTL lever signal and the range in proportion
- Dimension 45*20*15mm

13
TEMPERATURE SENSOR

The temperature sensor measures the amount of heat energy or even coldness that is generated an object or system, allowing us to "sense" or detect any physical change to that temperature producing either an analogue or digital output.

Here the LM35 is precision IC temperature sensor with its output proportional to the temperature (in °C) The sensor circuitry is sealed and therefore

it is not subjected to oxidation and other process. With LM35, temperature can be measured accurately than with a thermistor.

It also possess low self- heating and does not cause more than 0.1°C Temperature rise in still air.

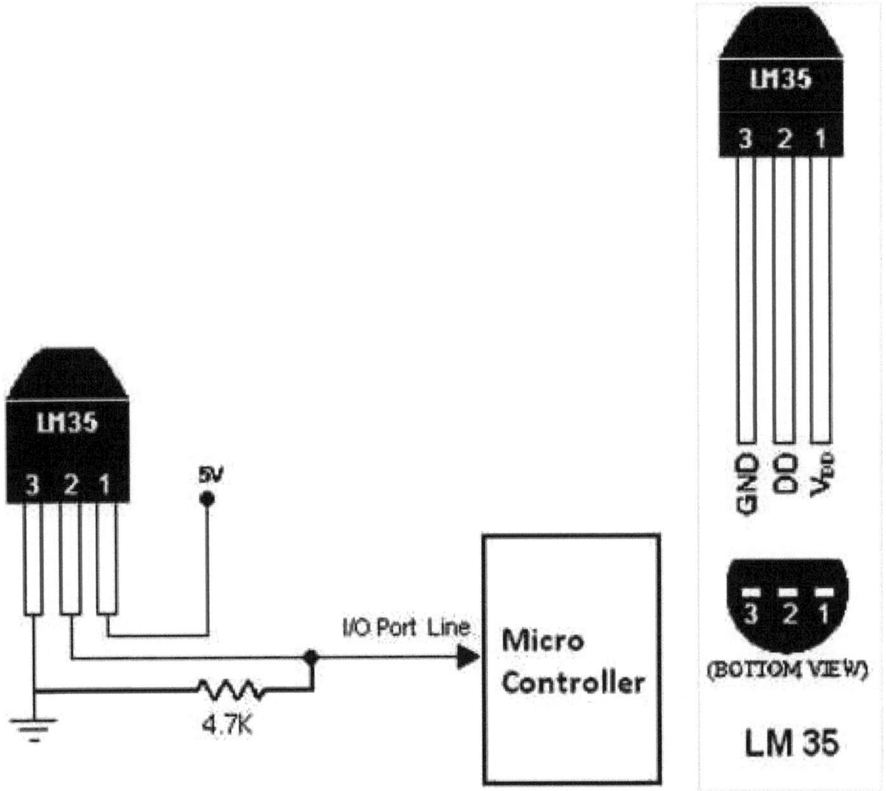

Fig 12. Temperature sensor

13.1 Features

- The operating temperature range is from -55°C to 150°C
- Calibrated directly in ° Celsius(centigrade)
- Linear +10.0 mV/°C scale factor
- Suitable for remote applications
- Operating voltage: 4V to 30V

13.2 Pin description:

Pin number	Function	Name
1	Supply voltage (+35V to -2V)	Vcc
2	output voltage (-6V to -1V)	output
3	Ground (0V)	ground

14

WATER PROBE OR HUMIDITY SENSOR

Humidity is the presence of water in air. The amount of water vapor in air can affect human comfort as well as many manufacturing processes in industries. The presence of water vapor also influences various physical, chemical, and biological processes.

Fig 13. Water of humidity sensor

14.1 Sensing Principle:

Humidity measurement can be done using dry and wet bulb hygrometers, dew point hygrometers, and electronic hygrometers. There has been a surge in the demand of electronic hygrometers, often called humidity sensors.

Electronic type hygrometers or humidity sensors can be broadly divided into two categories: one employs capacitive sensing principle, while other use resistive effects

14.2 Applications:

In medical applications, humidity control is required for respiratory equipment, sterilizers, incubators, pharmaceutical processing, and biological products. Humidity control is also necessary in chemical gas purification, dryers, ovens, film desiccation, paper and textile production, and food processing. In agriculture, measurement of humidity is important for plantation protection (dew prevention), soil moisture monitoring, etc.

15

Light-Dependent Resistor (LDR)

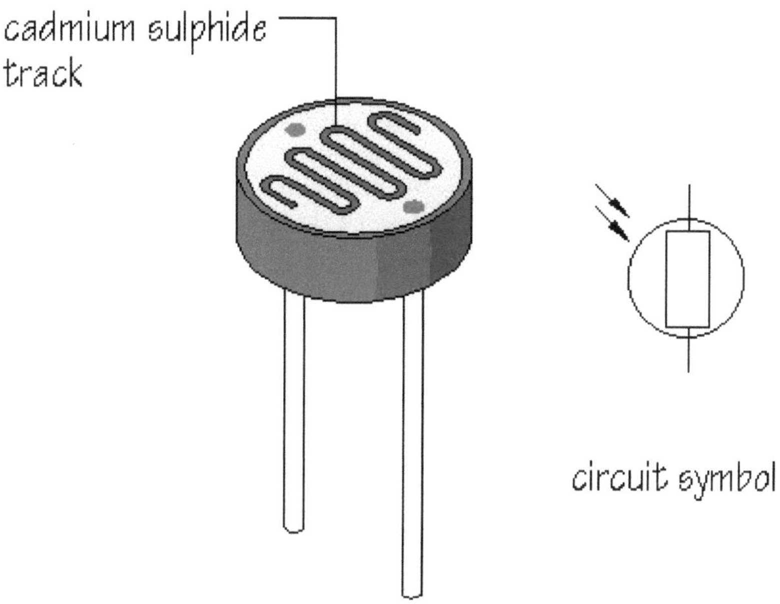

Fig 14. LDR sensor

A light-dependent resistor, alternatively called an LDR, photo resistor, photoconductor, or photocell, is a variable resistor whose value decreases with increasing incident light intensity.

An LDR is made of a high-resistance semiconductor. If light falling on the device is of high enough frequency, photons absorbed by the semiconductor give bound electrons enough energy to jump into the conduction band. The resulting free electron (and its hole partner) conduct electricity, thereby lowering resistance.

A photoelectric device can be either intrinsic or extrinsic. In intrinsic devices, the only available electrons are in the valence band, and hence the photon must have enough energy to excite the electron across the entire band gap. Extrinsic devices have impurities added, which have a ground state energy closer to the conduction band - since the electrons don't have as far to jump, lower energy photons (i.e. longer wavelengths and lower frequencies) are sufficient to trigger the device.

Two of its earliest applications were as part of smoke and fire detection systems and camera light meters. Because cadmium sulfide cells are inexpensive and widely available, LDRs are still used in electronic devices that need light

detection capability, such as security alarms, street lamps, and clock radios (Wikipedia 2005). A photo resistor or light dependent resistor (LDR) is a resistor whose resistance decreases with increasing incident light intensity; in other words, it exhibits photoconductivity.

A photo resistor is made of a high resistance semiconductor. If light falling on the device is of high enough frequency, photons absorbed by the semiconductor give bound electrons enough energy to jump into the conduction band. The resulting free electron (and its hole partner) conduct electricity, thereby lowering resistance.

A photoelectric device can be either intrinsic or extrinsic. An intrinsic semiconductor has its own charge carriers and is not an efficient semiconductor, for example, silicon.

In intrinsic devices the only available electrons are in the valence band, and hence the photon must have enough energy to excite the electron across the entire band gap. Extrinsic devices have impurities, also called dopants, added whose ground state energy is closer to the conduction band; since the electrons do not have as far to jump, lower energy photons (that is, longer wavelengths and lower frequencies) are sufficient to trigger the device. If a sample of silicon has some of its atoms replaced by phosphorus atoms (impurities), there will be extra electrons available for conduction. This is an example of an extrinsic semiconductor. Photo resistors are basically photocells.

16

PC Controlling

In this section, the PC is used for guiding and monitoring purpose. The direction of movements of robot is controlled by using through zig-bee Module. In the earlier they have used camera for take only the Pictures. But in our project, we used the video camera. Which will be capture the high resolution videos. Which will be fixed on the robot, where that live videos can be displayed into PC's monitor.

Here, live video signals are sent to receiving section and which will be displayed through PC. The required data's and information's are taken and receiving by giving a proper instruction to robot from PC(user).

Working

The signal received by the zig-bee receiver and through the level convertor interfacing unit; we can send the signal to the microcontroller, which is a programmable IC, where we can program it to control the motors according to the signal from the computer. The motor driven circuit improves the current capacity of the microcontroller. The encoder is to convert the microcontroller digital signal into frequency code and decoder is for the reverse operation of the same process. The level convertor in the computer is to convert the signal level of the microcontroller to the computer RS232 port.

The microcontroller is also programmed to sense the various type of sensors and send the signal to computer. We are using wireless transmitter in the camera to transmit the video signal. This is received by video capturing card and monitored in the computer through the tuner card. Thus we can monitor the situation and can control the robot reading the planet.

17

Hardware results

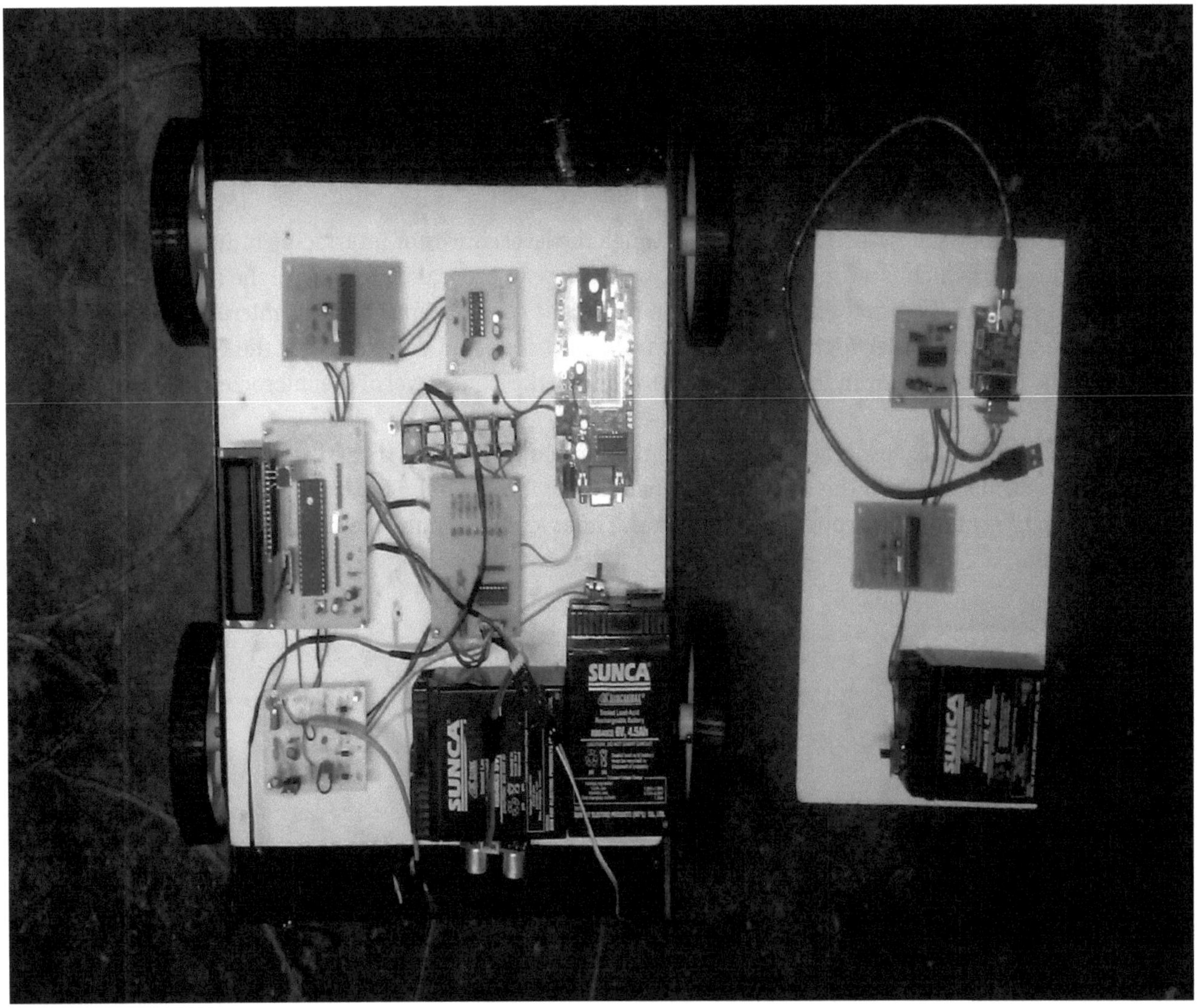

18

Cost Estimation

FACTOR	EXPENDITURE
GSM SIM 900A	1300
Ultrasonic Sensor	200
PIC Board & IC	200
Driver board	200
Zig-bee	1800
Robot base	2500
Battery	500
Motor	400
RS 232 to USB Cable	350
Water sensor	300
LDR	50
Wheel	200
TOTAL	**8,000**

19

APPENDIX

19.1 PROGRAMS:

```
#include<pic.h>
#include "HEADER.h"
/*****************************************************************
****/
CONFIG(HS & LVPDIS & WDTDIS & BOREN & UNPROTECT);
/*****************************************************************
****/
void delay(unsigned int de);
void condition_Checking_for_IR();
/*****************************************************************
****/
/*variable initailization*/
UBYTE
ser=0x37,st=0x01,st_1=0x01,data_cap=0x00,data_cap_1=0x00,check=0x00,val,
a,b,c,d,e,f,g,h,i,k,l,m,n,o,Xvalue,Yvalue,Zvalue;
bank2 UBYTE gsm_data[95];
UWORD gsm_count=0,check_sum,adc_value; UBYTE gsm[5],b1=0,a1=0;
UBYTE j=1;
//
UBYTE p,q;
unsigned int Count;
bit Initial_checking_flag = 0; bit Checking_flag_for_IR2 = 0;
bit delay_flag=0;
bit delay_flag_1=0;
unsigned int Timercount=0;
unsigned int Timer_Count_2;
unsigned int TimeCnt;
double PulseInTime=0;
/* variable calculating the echo travel time */
double cmDistance;
/* variable calculating the distance within limits */
unsigned int tDistance;
/* temperary variable for holding the distance value */
unsigned int TimeCnt=0;
/* timer0 overflow count */
```

```
/*************************************************************
****/
unsigned char htd(unsigned char value)
{
unsigned char msb=0, lsb=0;
msb = value & 0xF0; /* Filter for high byte */ msb = msb>>4;
lsb = value & 0x0F; /* Filter for low byte */ value=(msb*10)+lsb;
return value;
}
/************************************************************ unsigned char dth(unsigned char value)
{
unsigned char msb=0,lsb=0;
msb = value/10; /* Filter for high byte */
lsb = value%10; /* Filter for low byte */ value=(msb<<4)|lsb;
return value;
}
/*************************************************************
****/
void display(unsigned char k) // to display a two digit value
{
lcd_data(k/10+'0');// to display the tens value lcd_data(k%10+'0'); // to display the ones value
}
/*************************************************************
****/
void delay(unsigned int de)
{
while(de--);
}
/***********************************************************/
/************************************************************ void interrupt Timer0_ISR()
{
if(TMR0IF==1)
{
TimeCnt++;
TMR0IF=0;
}
if(RCIF==1)
{ RCIF=0;
q=1;
p=RCREG;
}
/*void interrupt serial()
{
if(RCIF==1)
{
buffer[i]=RCREG;
i++;
}
```

```
}*/
}
/************************************************************ void interrupt Timer1_ISR()
{
if(TMR1IF==1)
{
TMR1IF=0;
TimeCnt++;
}
}
/************************************************************/
/************************************************************/ void Delay10Us() /* Delay function for 10 micro-sec */
{
int dCnt;
for(dCnt=0;
dCnt<3;
dCnt++);
}
/************************************************************/
/*void interrupt ser()//SENT TO CNT
{
}
*/
void TriggerPulse()//16pin
{
RC1=0;
TRISC2=0; /* pulse signal line made O/P for trigger */ Delay10Us();
RC1=1; /* H_to_L transition. ie, Trigger Pulse to the Ultrasonic range finder module */
Delay10Us(); RC1=0;
/* T2CON=0x01;
CCP2CON=0x0C;
PR2=0xF9;
CCPR2L=0x80;
TMR2=0;
TRISC2=0;
TMR2ON=1;*/
TMR0 = 0;
TimeCnt=0; /* clear timer overflow count, pulseIn time and timer register count */
PulseInTime=0;
}
/************************************************************/ void PulseInMode(void)//23pin
{
RC0=0; /* clear I/O pin */
TRISC0=1; /* pulse signal line made I/P for echo PulseIn ULTRASONIC TO CNT */
//while(!RC0); /* wait for PulseIn signal to go HIGH */ T0CS=0; /* start echo PulseIn timer */
while(RC0); /* wait for PulseIn signal to go LOW */ T0CS=1; /* stop echo PulseIn timer */
RC0 =0; /* clear I/O pin */
PulseInTime= TMR0; /* timer calculations [return time in Us] */
```

```
PulseInTime= (double)(((PulseInTime* 0.2) + (TimeCnt * 51.2)));
cmDistance = (double) PulseInTime/58;
/* timer value in Us divided by
58 gives the cm distance */
tDistance =(unsigned int)cmDistance;
/* display of the calculated distance */
if(tDistance >=11 && tDistance <=34)
{
//RC0=0;
//lcd_command(0x80);
//lcd_display("OBSTACLE SEARCH.",16);
//lcd_command(0xc0);
//lcd_display("LOAD STATUS:-OFF",16);
//display(Count);
}
else if(tDistance <=10)
{
se=1;
//RC0=1;
//lcd_command(0xC0);
//delay(100);
//lcd_display(" OBS DETECT ",16);
//delay(60000);
//lcd_command(0xC0);
delay(100);
/*lcd_display(" ",16); TXREG='2';
delay(5000); Right_motf=0; Left_motf=0;
Right_motr=0;
Left_motr=0;
lcd_command(0x01); delay(100);
lcd_display("LOAD STATUS:- ON",16); delay(100000);
RD2 = 0;
delay(100000); RD2 = 1;
delay(100000);*/
}
}
void main()
{
delay(100);
Serial_Init(9600);
Port_init();
lcd_init();
Timercount=0;
Timer_Count_2=0;
TMR0=0;
PSA= 1; T0CS=1;
T0IF=0;
T0IE=1;
```

```
Serial_Conout("ok",2);
lcd_command(0x01);
lcd_command(0x80);
lcd_display(" WELCOME L6",16);
delay(60000);
delay(60000);
lcd_command(0X01);
Receive(1);
while(1)
{
TriggerPulse(); // Trigger mode PulseInMode();
// PulseIn mode se=0;
CHS0=0; //FOR 1 CHANNEL SELECT CHS1=0;
CHS2=0;
ADON=1;
delay(200);
ADCON0=ADCON0|0X04;
delay(200);
adc_value=ADRESH;
adc_value=adc_value<<8;
adc_value=(adc_value+ADRESL)/0x02;
Tem=adc_value;
delay(100);
adcconvert();
lcd_command(0x8e);
delay(100);
//lcd_data(g+0x30); lcd_data(e+0x30); lcd_data(b+0x30);
CHS0=1;
//FOR 2 CHANNEL SELECT CHS1=0;
CHS2=0;
ADON=1;
delay(200);
ADCON0=ADCON0|0X04;
delay(200);
adc_value=ADRESH;
adc_value=adc_value<<8;
adc_value=(adc_value+ADRESL)/0x02;
Soil=adc_value;
delay(100);
adcconvert();
lcd_command(0xc0);
delay(100);
lcd_data('S');
lcd_data(g+0x30);
lcd_data(e+0x30);
lcd_data(b+0x30);
CHS0=0; //FOR 3 CHANNEL SELECT CHS1=1;
CHS2=0;
```

```
ADON=1;
delay(200);
ADCON0=ADCON0|0X04;
delay(200);
adc_value=ADRESH;
adc_value=adc_value<<8;
adc_value=(adc_value+ADRESL)/0x02;
LDR=adc_value;
delay(100); adcconvert();
lcd_command(0xc5); delay(100); lcd_data('L'); lcd_data(g+0x30); lcd_data(e+0x30); lcd_data(b+0x30);
if(q==1)
{
q=0;
{
if(p=='5')
Right_motf=1;
Left_motf=1;
Right_motr=1;
Left_motr=1;
lcd_command(0xC0);
delay(100);
lcd_display(" STOP ",16);
delay(65000);
lcd_command(0xC0);
delay(100);
lcd_display(" ",16);
//lcd_command(0x01);
delay(100);
}
if((p=='8')&&(se==0))
{
Right_motf=0;//(f)
Left_motf=0; Right_motr=1;
Left_motr=1;
lcd_command(0xC0);
delay(100);
lcd_display(" FORWARD ",16);
delay(65000);
lcd_command(0xC0);
delay(100);
lcd_display(" ",16);
//lcd_command(0x01);
} if(p=='2')
{
Right_motf=1;
//(r) Left_motf=1;
Right_motr=0;
Left_motr=0;
```

```
lcd_command(0xC0);
delay(100);
lcd_display(" REVERSE ",16); delay(65000); lcd_command(0xC0); delay(100);
lcd_display(" ",16);
//lcd_command(0x01);
}
if(p=='4')
{
Right_motf=1;
//(le) Left_motf=0;
Right_motr=0;
Left_motr=1;
lcd_command(0xC0);
delay(100);
lcd_display(" LEFT ",16);
delay(65000); lcd_command(0xC0); delay(100);
lcd_display(" ",16);
//lcd_command(0x01);
}
if(p=='6')
{
Right_motf=0;
//(ri) Left_motf=1;
Right_motr=1;
Left_motr=0; lcd_command(0xC0); delay(100);
lcd_display(" RIGHT ",16); delay(65000); lcd_command(0xC0); delay(100);
lcd_display(" ",16);
//lcd_command(0x01);
}
}
if(Tem>40)
{
lcd_command(0x80); delay(100);
lcd_display("TEMP Obnormal",13); delay(2000);
}
if(Tem<40)
{
}
if(Soil>200)
{
Serial_Conout("TEMP Obnormal",13);
Triper=1;
delay(100);
msg_sendtemp();
delay(1000);
Triper=0;
lcd_command(0x80);
delay(100);
```

```
lcd_display("Temp normal ",13);
delay(2000);
lcd_command(0xC0);
delay(100);
lcd_display("H2O Detected ",13);
delay(2000);
Serial_Conout("H2O Detected",13);
Triper=1;
delay(60000);
msg_sendsoil();
delay(1000);
Triper=0;
}
}
}
/***********************************************************/
```

20
Conclusion

In this book,wireless communication between robot and wireless base station. The main task of this project was two parts to program the Pic microcontroller on the both the base station and robot interfaced to the Zig- Bee module which would enable us to wireless control the robot and to measure the atmospheric conditions and the researching the other planet to get various information and data analyzing continuously. This level of completion was successfully tested and parameters were also measured.

9 798886 411409

Printed by Libri Plureos GmbH in Hamburg,
Germany